A Day Like Today

A Day Like Today

Barbara Henning

Negative Capability PRESS
MOBILE, ALABAMA

A Day Like Today

Cover Art and Author Photo by Cliff Fyman
Editing by Rachael Fowler
Interior Design by Megan Cary

ISBN 978-0942544-76-3
Library of Congress Control Number: 2015903376

Negative Capability Press
62 Ridgelawn Drive East
Mobile, Alabama 36608
(251) 591-2922

www.negativecapabilitypress.org
facebook.com/negativecapabilitypress

ACKNOWLEDGEMENTS

These poems were composed from daily one page journal entries written in 2012. Many thanks to the *New York Times* writers (2012) for words and phrases collaged into the poems. Much appreciation for love and support from my family and friends, especially Dumisani Kambi-Shamba, Greg Snyder and my children, Linnée Snyder and Michah Saperstein. Special thanks to Miranda Maher, Lewis Warsh, Cliff Fyman, Sue Walker, Rachael Fowler, Megan Cary, and to the editors of the journals and magazines that published these poems—*6x6, BlazeVOX, Boog City, Brooklyn Paramount, Brooklyn Rail, Clash of the Lichens, Downtown Brooklyn, House Organ, Hydrogen Jukebox, LIUFF Arts & Leisure, Marguerite Avenue, Negative Capability, Otter Magazine, Rampike Magazine, Salzburg Review, Soluable Edge, Spiral Orb, Talisman, Tuesday Poem (Dusie),* and *Visceral Brooklyn.*

For Luke, Logan, and Kayin.

TABLE OF CONTENTS

WINTER

FALL

WINTER

WINTER

UP EARLY PEDDLING

Up early peddling against
the wind, swerving around
trucks and cars unloading
beer and children. To have
an original idea is to swerve
or so says Mr. Foreman,
and on Third Street I glide
over the bumpy patched up
pavement until I cross
Broadway, then make
a smooth left through
a housing complex, chain up
my bike at Houston and
Wooster and at 9:15 ring
the bell. For several weeks
last year, the Earth was
surrounded by an extra
ring of radiation, highly
charged particles swerving
around the planet. In front
of the mirror with Genny
leading, we synchronize
our movements, moving
into stillness, a charged
room full of human triangles.

STRANGE AFTERNOON DREAM

Strange afternoon dream
about an English department chair—
the old time male type—
who hires me to take his place.
Apple could hire 3,000 foreigners
overnight and convince them to live
in dormitories. It's full steam
ahead for Mickey Mouse in India.
A slippery rich politician is selling
a bill of goods. Just answer my
correspondence, and see to my
appointments. Need a new mattress
to go with that TV? You're in
the right place. I forget something
outside, a cabinet now covered
with mud. While I'm scraping it,
the chair's watching me from
another window, shaking his finger.
There's always been disagreement
on these American shores as to
just what the "best" English is.
I'm thinking, oh this is how it's done
and then I'm piloting an airplane
out of there. Falling asleep now
with my pen resting on its side
and this little blob of ink, growing.

BEFORE THE NOON HOUR

Nine minutes and a half before
the noon hour and the republican
already has his feet in Iowa
and his eye on Florida.
Biking four long blocks uphill
in the fierce cold, I'm thankful
I was born with a fibula in both legs.
While the candidate wears
a herring-bone cashmere tuxedo
with men's fabrications,
my face is wrapped in wool
so thick I can't see over
my shoulder. The athlete
is the fastest man on no legs,
his j shaped prostheses barely
touch the ground. Decorated
with a tattoo: I do not run
like a man running aimlessly.
I peddle steadily homeward.
In the mail, a surgeon's bill for
Barbra Hennig from NYU Hospital
for 15,500 dollars, a hysterectomy
I never had. You're missing
an "a" and an "n," I say to the voice
at the 800 number. And today
I still have my uterus. A new
system is on it's way, they say,
one that will eliminate these
kinds of errors as well as
the need for insurance companies.

OUR SKY IS *OUR* SKY

Billboards along the BQE take up
a lot of sky. On a day like today,
we lose green but gain U.S.
unarmed aircraft protection—
But, it's *our* sky, says Al-Asadi.
Up above the branches, down below
the tree digester spits out
bits and pieces to warm the earth
and plants through the winter freeze.
Encased in wood, metal and cement,
our bodies rarely nourish anything.
One and only one republican
has been given protection
from the elements and *this*
is designed to cement his image
as a front-runner. Safe inside—
the traffic sounds like the tide,
a car door slamming and instead
of seabirds, the twitter of voices
on the street and the sound of air,
quietly and continually filling
and leaving my lungs while upstairs
love bangs the bed against the wall.

UP THE HUDSON

Up the Hudson, the dry leafless
trees tower around the cabin.
At best, we are less than halfway
through the task of indexing
all plants, fungi and algae on earth.
A willowy silence. Dorothy watches
TV in her bedroom, a show about
an 850 pound woman, hidden
in her home, inside her massive
flesh. Usually, we are surrounded
by city sounds, musicians whistling,
bouncing balls and human-animal
sounds. Here birds call to each other
and the rustle of dry plants scatter
over the path. Why don't you lock
this place up, I say, and come back
to the city? A moment of televised
silence. Sudden pangs and strange
sounds with no obvious cause.
Dorothy clears her throat. Barbie,
you want to go now? Why are
the trees so tall and skinny? I ask.
Because there isn't a lot of soil,
very quickly rock bottom.

AT SUNRISE

Instead of meditating, I mop
the floors and hallways.
To prevent downloading free
music, Dutch cable companies
obtain a court order to block
access to the pirate bay.
In fancy gyms across the city,
people steal from each other,
yuppie-on-yuppie crime
while musicians and night
workers seek the quiet dim
of dark apartments. At sunset,
I switch on the parking lights
and run upstairs to pee,
hoping the police won't
notice. Then I circle around
block after block, finally
finding a tiny spot between
B and C, in front of the yuppie
building with a doorman,
a doorman's sole purpose,
so they say, to provide security.

1200 OLD SHOES

Sent to an Indonesian Court
with a message: Let the boy
go free. Outside, a big truck
down shifts as the tree tops
tremble in the wind. So
he stole the shoes of a
policeman. He needed them,
and in about five billion
years, it won't matter.
The planet earth will be
engulfed by the expanding
radius of the sun. Martine
and I walk to Angelica
to see *Melancholia,* an
out-of-orbit planet heading
toward earth, and everyone
still going about their lives,
shopping. Build a magic
circle, the woman tells
the little boy, and hold your
hands over it. As the planet
breaks through the gravity
shield, the electricity snaps
and boom, just like that—
all the beauty and mean
pettiness is over and done.

UPSIDE DOWN

Bankruptcy lawyers
often steer black debtors
into disastrous Chapter 13.
My love calls and wants
to make amends. You were
right. It *was* about race.
So let's look for someone
more in the shade. We
need contrasts, says
the candidate, not just
a paler shade of what
we have. Today is the 600th
anniversary of the birth
of Joan of Arc, the cross-
dressing, teenage virgin-
warrior-martyr-saint.
You know, dear, women
are not interchangeable.
On the bike route home,
trucks keep cutting in front,
pushing me into traffic.
Wearing high heels can be
dangerous, especially
on a bike. Sometimes
the dangerous way is
the safest bet and the road
to zero excess growth
will ride up and down
quite a few more times.
I close my eyes and listen.
When I drift out of sync,
you may realign me
by briefly tapping on my
shoulder, then this mind-
body will drift into sleep.

I WAKE UP LATE

I wake up late and groggy
looking around the room
at Rosemary Mayer's
orange and yellow circles.
They pair off and make
circles within circles, a chain
of duets. How close we once
were, luck, lady duck, that piece
of high desert drift wood
from the Coyote wilderness.
Lewis's collages, hours clipping
and pasting the letter O.
You can follow the process
as the outer blue circles
float above. I drink a glass
of water and recall an old
woman at the Y swimming
in the lane beside me. Her twin
sister, she said, was much
healthier than she was and
it was all because she drank
a lot of water. Interests change,
social circles shift, a family
moves away. I drink another
glass of water. Always the same
memory pushing its way
to the surface, hunched over
and swimming lap after lap.

NIGHT AFTER NIGHT

Night after night,
over and over,
pulling up the covers,
turning on the light,
and my first thought
when I get into bed
is how lucky I am
to have this place,
these covers and
to be here right now.

IN THE DARK

A 540-year-old bank in Tucsan
of Siena mislead regulators
about a secret derivative contract
later found in a safe. That's too
calculating and my ex isn't like that.
Sir Isaac Newton once said he could
calculate the motions of the heavenly
bodies, but not the madness of people.
All my receipts are scrambled.
I want to be meticulous, but keep
finding something I skipped.
I want to wake up but my hands
are on my aunt's back, and after
all that upright beauty, she slumps
into a blur. It's the passing and losing
that's so crushing. With the storm
today trading volumes were a little
thinner than usual. Slipping back
into dream—he's so excited that
he does a handstand without touching
the ground, simultaneously smoking
a cigarette. I drift off again, then
wake up at 3 a.m. aching for love.

MULTIPLE CHOICE

Wrote a multiple choice exam
for my love, kind of funny
but serious, too. Later, we talk
and I'm going to see him soon,
but only as friends. Obama calls
for gun control legislation
and gun happy folks are disturbed.
Some of my family and friends
will be worried. If those in power
are serious about the poverty trap,
they should be serious, too,
about not setting it up in the first place.
I just want to see him as friends
even though it's true that I am
still in love with him. This morning
a very sweet yoga teacher,
a young man, held my hand
in his and said, you have such
a nice practice. Why are some
destined to be alone and others
with long time companions—
My bookshelves with hundreds,
maybe thousands of books—
these are my trusted advisors
and enthusiastic companions.

AND THIS IS HOW IT GOES

Out on Long Island playing
with the boys when my love
texts with a question— Where
should he go in the East Village
to buy a bicycle for his son?
An ordinary question. Ordinary
people in Tibet have taken
to the streets to rally against
Chinese authorities. Self-
immolations. Luke and Logan
chase me, laughing hysterically.
In the past month, at least
twenty-two children have died
in camps in Kabul. Research
suggests that American parents
become less happy once
the first child arrives. Logan
says, Push me, Gramma. Luke
says, Push me into the sky.
Higher and higher and even
higher. Never stop, Gramma, never.
And this is how the joy spreads.

PERHAPS WE CAN JUST
TURN OFF

Men's voices talking outside
my window and cars swishing by
on Avenue A. The light blue sky.
It's supposed to be warmer today.
No do-this-do-that thoughts. Push
them away. Swish and someone
turns over in a bed upstairs. Below
me a soundtrack fills Jacqueline's
almost empty apartment and I am
suspended above it. In China,
Xiou climbs to the top of a mountain
with her illegal cell phone to call
her parents over the border.
Maybe now that the familiar bed
isn't an option, we'll talk on the phone
about race and our relationship
or about race in *The Scarlet Letter*
and the Native Americans
on the fringe. Perhaps we can
just turn off the location tagging
for once by simply clicking
on the *other* box under identity.

APPLAUSE

Luke split his lip today
and had to get six stitches
The court has all but ruled out
a split primary. We're lucky
we're here together for
however long we have.
Victory sends the sold-out
crowd of more than 6,700
fans to their feet. At the very
top of their game, there has
to be something spiritual
about our existence, the way
we're so carefully designed
but can't fathom why or how.
Hoping to win a long-futile battle
against falling prices,
all our speculation adds up
to these religions. So here
we are falling down,
then getting up again, running
down the block and losing
every single person ever
nearby and in our arms.

SINGING SO LOUDLY

Most of Occupy
has gone into retreat,
but their ideas are still
advancing. Once Tenney
asked me to teach yoga
to Zen students on retreat.
I like being singular,
easily get group-itus
so I passed. Often
we cannot talk outside
first-person singular,
devoted as we are
to our particular interests,
like fine Oriental carpets.
Today I stop in front
of a dogwood tree
with glossy leaves
orange seeds and berries.
The tree is full of
chirping birds with brown
swashes on their faces.
And I wonder if
they are cold and maybe
that's why they are
clustered together like that
and singing so loudly.

HERE WE ARE

Off to the stationery store on Avenue A
to buy paper and metal bookends.
At least 58 people died in Europe
this week in a brutal cold wave,
plunging temperatures to 17 degrees
below zero. When I step inside,
I'm suddenly phlegmy and coughing.
Blood starts pouring out of my
left nostril. A funny old woman
hidden inside a blue hooded coat
darts out the door. Republicans
point at the millions of immigrant
workers pouring into the country.
Then I look in the mirror and see
a funny looking old woman
with her head wrapped
like a mummy and a tissue stuck
in her nose. King Tut's mummy
was recently removed from
the sarcophagus, and placed
in a climate-controlled box
to be displayed at a museum in Luxor.
My husband often had a bloody nose.
Maybe we'll find each other
in another life. When I think of
losing my children, I feel my body
crack into pieces. China's cracking
down on subversive meditating
disciples of the Dalai Lama.
Be thankful for now, Barbara.
Today. This minute. Here we are.

RAMONA SAYS

Ramona says don't lose another
pound, and I say, it's out of
my control. She suggests
eating fish and I say, Never,
but if I have to—before death—
of course, I will. So many
vegetables in the spectrum
of green and gold. When people
say something negative,
it sometimes stays around
reappearing later. A train crash
in Buenos Aires leaves
at least five hundred people
injured. Skinny, too skinny,
the spectrum of morning light
necessary to trigger a positive
circadian response and most
effective in the long blue-green
range. Maybe some folks solidly
into a project don't hear those
voices, but I do. Jumping into
ice might sound like a great idea
after a grueling workout. Today
rain comes down in little ice pelts.
Oh February, go away!

LIKE BIRDS

*The Girl with the Dragon
Tattoo* is a suspenseful
mystery with a dynamo
young actress as punk sniper
brain tough beauty. The film
is an excuse to watch her.
A Ukrainian coal-mining
dynamo dug a record 102 tons,
single-handedly, in a single
shift in 1935. The silver-gray
crocodile boot from Reed
Krakoff is sophisticated
and tough and that's tops.
The republican plan of action
is step one, drill, step two,
drill and step three, keep drilling.
At a slight distance, people
seem to trill like birds, personal
tragedy sometimes interfering
with seeing, recognizing, hearing.
Researchers have found
that avian infidelity is more
common in severe or uncertain
weather. And that's no excuse
for being fashionably late.

I WAS WALKING DOWN

I was walking down Avenue A
and across Houston when
I thought, Why are we here?
Wallace Stevens found inspiration
on his daily walk, but we walk
differently in high heels.
A woman is crazy in love
with a sedate purple dress
with black velvet flower appliqués
and the crazy weather continues.
In Europe people are freezing
to death and yesterday it snowed
in Libya. Still a prolonged
intellectual tussle over the climate.
In 2005 the global ringtone
market reached its height
and Crazy Frog is still worth $2.2
billion dollars. We get close,
fall in love and then bye-bye.
The winner gets a crushed fedora.

OUTSIDE POET'S HOUSE

Outside Poet's House,
smaller than snowflakes,
two girls in blue and a dog
run with the fierce wind.
Some mammals are smaller
in hotter climates. A big grey
cloud moves south and the wind
blows north while under foot,
a brown seed pod. A U-haul
turns onto River Terrace
and stops behind the Salvation
Army truck with its engine
running and a guy inside
drinking from a paper cup.
The wind blows a blue plastic
ground cover into ripples
and the sun glimmers on
the surface of the river.
Consequences continue
to ripple outward while
trillions of snow flakes swirl
with the wind, the bedrock
a few feet underfoot. Across
the river, New Jersey is
a multi-level lego project.

WHEN I WAS IN MOSCOW

I had typhoid fever. Willie
Lincoln died of typhoid fever,
but I only lost twenty pounds.
At St. Marks, Frances Richard
reads abstract sound poems,
trilling, she trills. Then I read
with sentences and paragraphs,
a life of twigs and sticks. Later
I crawl into bed and dream
about baby wasps developing
inside living flies, feeding
on their tissues. When they
reach adult size, they crawl out
of the dying bodies of their hosts.
Adele's success is burning up
the press, reaching a feverish
pitch. The older generation
is dying and soon we step in line.
The floor expands from the reverb
below— my down-stairs neighbor
Jackie dancing. A reverb box
yields an eerie electronic timbre,
something like a late-night
train sound. When I look down
at my leg and my silk slip,
I imagine my love asleep
beside me, his hand on my hip.

ON THE BOTTOM RUNG

Logan slips on the bottom rung
of the slide. He stands up and starts
to cry. Looking at me, he frowns
and says, Gramma, I'm *always*
falling down. Some say hitting
bottom is a prelude to a rebound.
Fleas were ten times bigger
then and their mouths were
sharp enough to feed on dinosaurs.
Our mouths, teeth and tongues are
orchestrated to enunciate the inner
and the outer. Crouched down,
Patti Smith is naked and clutching
the top rung of a radiator while
staring directly into Mapplethorpe's
camera. The strange and sulky
beauty of always. A reflection
of gas flames from the fireplace,
flickering on the window
as the planet moves closer and closer
to the end of its life span—
this ravishingly beautiful earth.

WE AMERICANS

The American captain in *Benito*
Cereno is optimistic and his point
of view promotes self interest.
On the evil bible website there's
all the justification anyone needs
for murder and mayhem. Our education
system can be a powerful mechanism
for the reproduction of privilege.
Trying to keep my view positive—
while red squirrels tunnel through
the snow with ease, I stumble
through the subway tunnels
with a terrible cough and difficulty
breathing. To teach yoga is
to transmit energy. But American
literature? Even if the body
is listless, sitting at a desk,
there's always some energy coiling
inside and a transmission line
capable of transferring enough qi
for hundreds of thousands of cells.

A HOUSE ON FIRE

can mesmerize and make
your heart race. The tall
African man beside me is
absorbed in prep postures
and meditation. Under his
do-rag his dreds are turning
grey. His feet remind me of
my love. The famous feathered
dinosaur archaeopteryx
seems to have had a penchant
for fossilizing in painful
positions, but this guy is
very flexible and he has
beautiful eyes. When he's
resting, I imagine crawling
beside him and making fire.
Hackers record our
keystrokes and passwords,
grab screenshots and even
crawl from one machine
to another. This economy
might not be flexible
enough to absorb these
economic shocks, so carefully
I roll up my mat, bow
to my friend and head home.
The window's open as if
it's summer and it isn't,
as if it's bedtime and tonight
these words are much too
slippery to cuddle up with.

ON SATURDAY

On the fleeting day
of a big wave,
two passenger trains
in Poland collide
at high speed,
killing sixteen people,
and I fall asleep
deeply, dreaming
that Allen is alive
and well. I tell him
I have been looking
all over for him.
Where have you
been? He says,
I thought you
didn't want to
find me. Then
we cuddle up
in the passenger
side of a van
heading downtown
on Gratiot Avenue.

THESE SOCKS

These socks cost $10 a pair
and the darning spool has
been in my sewing box for years.
Finally I sit down and begin
weaving. No room for straying
thoughts, just in and out,
across and over. Then I walk
through the park with my
camera, reaching out to smooth
a stray hair, a spool of genes
blowing in the wind, a leaf,
a rock, a branch, a twig,
my reflection in a puddle,
pants too short, high water
with striped socks and these
clodhopper clogs. Santana
gives up two hits and one
walk while getting two
strikeouts. Two minus two
and a quarter. Still a little
behind. As Kierkegaard
noted, life is lived forward
but understood backward,
a darn good reason for
making the rich pay more.

IN A FRACTIONAL WAY

My father was a man
who loved me as long as
I did what he wanted.
Democrats in New York State
outnumber republicans
two to one, yet republicans
hold a narrow majority
in the state senate. Wearing
a hooded sweatshirt,
sunglasses and holding
a bag of candy, Trayvon
Martin was fatally shot
in Florida on February 28th.
A pair of eerily lifelike
oil pumps on an empty lot
at 8th Avenue and 46th.
Just want to be quiet now.
An ambitious project
anyhow to save every
book and every memory.
Crowds line up—some
in the rain—to get an iPad.
Standing here with my camera
and my pad of paper.
Be simple. Be a witness.

THE M14 BUS

The M14 bus crawls around
a construction site and then
crosses 7th Avenue. A father
is reading a book, his right
arm around his daughter,
his hand covering her mouth.
How long is a fraction
of a second? Her long blond
hair, beautiful, maybe six
or seven, red finger nail polish
on one hand only, pink tights.
The pupil gets larger and darker.
Depress the shutter to advance
the narrative. He removes
his hand and she pulls it back,
leaning into the book.
Suddenly his hand is moving
and she looks up, smiling.
One front tooth gone,
a big red gap. The courting
crow has an iridescent pair
of long narrow tail feathers.
Above a grey sky, fog
and winter clouds. Researchers
have found a tiny fraction
of heavy metals in the fog
along the western North
American coastline. I cover
my mouth with my scarf
and walk west into the wind.

SPRING

A DAY LIKE TODAY

My love wants to stop by
and suddenly he's here.
He misses me he says
and he wants to try
again. It's as if we've
been together without
interruption. I want to
believe him and even
though the word of
the day is forestall,
the eggs in the Hawk
nest are high up and
a baby hawk is pecking
its way to daylight.
We hold each other
quietly, then walk
around a big flowering
pear tree at the 8th Street
entrance to the park,
the bodies of the trees
leaning this and that way,
relaxing into darkness,
just as we were
minutes earlier
in the dusk-dim light.

A BLIND SPOT

is simply an obscuration
of the visual field. I try
to memorize the potholes
in the dark as I bike over
to Trader Joe's in the rain.
Two lines snake up and down
the aisles from the door
to the checkout. I shop
in line, moving from one
aisle to the next, picking
groceries off the shelves.
In front of me, a blind
woman maybe late thirties
with a big sandy seeing
eye dog. She's holding
the leash with one hand
and her other hand is on
the shoulder of a very old
woman, maybe eighty,
stooped over and pushing
a stroller with two babies,
maybe eight-month old
twins. Touch, patience
and sheer determination
and we follow the neon lights
back out into the rain.

WHITE BLOSSOMS

A motorcycle idles
at the light, a tattooed
man adjusts his backpack
and my new friend
Leon and I walk
to the park as I roll
my bike along beside us.
We eat lunch, lettuce,
tomatoes on wheat bread
with tahini. Then
Leon tells me that
he has thyroid cancer
and won't take any AMA
medicine. He should
have been dead by now,
but with intense yoga
for twelve years,
he's still here.
We part on 7th Street
under a flowering
pear tree and then
we wander on home
in our own directions.
When the tulips are
finally ready to flower
underground tubers
will send up a second leaf.

C U IN 5 MINUTES

I'm sleeping when my phone
beeps with a text message:
At bus stop. c u in 5 minutes.
Sent to the wrong person
so I climb back into dream sleep.
As I am lying on my side,
my love climbs on top,
the blanket between us.
My heart starts to ache.
He forgot to take his hat
yesterday. Like a butterfly
folding its wings around
a small flower, taking,
then gone. He killed love,
Jeanie said. And that's
a crime. Then he texts me,
c u wednesday. Butterfly
wings are not just beautiful.
They are also sophisticated
collectors of solar energy.

OPTIMISM

Left my yoga mat some
where, maybe in the nail
shop or in the park, left
my water bottle and bracelet
at the yoga studio, my debit
card in the atm machine.
At least I didn't leave
my favorite scarf anywhere
this week. Woke up from
a brief nap, a little teary,
about something someone
said to me. You're too thin
skinned that's why you're
so negative. One of my
admirers. The skin of a
fresh pea is translucent
and slightly tough, a more
delicate version of the
covering on a fava bean.
Inside its skin are two
pieces that fall apart when
the skin is removed. At
the nail shop on First Ave
the young Chinese woman
marvels at the skin on
my legs. How many years?
Sixty-three? Oh my, they
look twenty-three. When
my finger knocks one gauge
off kilter, a tiny motor whirrs
and just like that the device
snaps back into position.

IF THERE REALLY IS

If there really is a war against
women, if New York State were
to embrace wind power, if we
were to close the Indian Point
nuclear plant for good—They
say that older animals typically
have less qi, but when I am
with Luke and Logan, they say,
Hi Gramma and I spin into their
make believe world. We rub
our hands together and pull
them apart, to feel the power,
to sing, run, cook and dance.
In the mind of a troll everything
is changeable. Over time
the *Times* reports that Americans
seem to have stopped caring
about each other. The Buffett
inspired rule would require
those making over one
million dollars to pay 30 percent
of their income in taxes. I meet
Georgia for lunch. She has a
brace on her neck. We talk as if
no time has passed. And we both
agree that life is better with a lover.

WHEN I GIVE AN EXAM

When I give an exam to my class
Vincent secretly copies from
wikipedia, something he could
easily have written himself. Revise it,
I say. Then I ride my bike from
Union Square to Thompson Street.
Windy with pollen everywhere.
Others swell up and sneeze,
but I cough. While large slow
moving storms send one swell
after another across the Midwest,
a group of tourists with suitcases
follows a guide leading them
into a bar for mojitos. If you don't
protect your intellectual invention,
if it's any good, it will be copied
almost immediately. The tourists
look at us on the sidewalk while
a political peacock with faded
plumage is still preening and
campaigning in North Carolina,
shuffling pointlessly through a zoo.

MADAGASCAR

I'm watching *Madagascar*
with the boys—hilarious
hip city zoo animals end up
in Africa but long to come
home to the Central Park Zoo.
With the emergence of zoos,
pet keeping and animal toys,
John Berger explains that animals
were slowly disappearing from
our daily lives. When the boys
take a bath, Luke stretches his
long young thin body under
the warm water and we play
with little action figures
and plastic frogs. Then I put
my feet into the tub, singing
row row row your boat gently
down the stream. Later
it's raining and we're together
under an umbrella, walking
through the park. Surely,
radioactive ocean water
from the Fukushima Daiichi
nuclear plant will migrate
around the globe and even if we
don't die this year, we will
all die eventually, so for now,
let's hold each other loosely.

ACCIDENTALLY

When he absorbed some LSD
through his fingertips, Abbie
Hoffman accidentally
discovered its mind-altering
qualities. To read is to
put my map alongside
someone else's and analyze
how and where we deviate.
When I took LSD and other
psychedelics, my map wandered
off course. How tired I am
sometimes of mapping my map.
Little squeaks in the kitchen.
I should try to catch that mouse
or fill in the holes. Bought
a big let-live trap, with a maze,
but he won't go inside. Last
night I realized that my love
and I are starting to make a three
dimensional body between us.
If you get too close, the actor
says, I'll be gone like a cool
breeze. At the end of the day,
a big black car passes by
with windows open, playing
loud Jewish Passover music.

BACK TO BROOKLYN

After my love pedals
his Rolls back to Brooklyn,
I am alone with a dream
and another lover who's
doing an amazing martial
art thing, rolling across
the floor at angles—Oh
I can't do that I say–I don't
have any fat on my spine.
Then several times we're
ready to fly in an airplane,
but I can't find my bag
or my jacket. I'm very
inconspicuous until
the airplane becomes
a weird air balloon
and I realize that I left
everything at a party
with a lot of children.
Up above the balloon
becomes a helicopter rising
above me and I'm standing
in the middle of a big green
lawn surrounded by groves
of maples and sycamores.

THE EAST RIVER

The river laps and overlaps,
as runners, cars and trucks
pass by. Are we on
the 10th Street Bridge?
my friend Carol asks. Yes,
I say, definitively. But
both bridges, she says,
have the same dip and
a puddle in exactly
the same place. We
examine the coincidental
puddle, and then upon
crossing discover that
coming and going we
were on the 6th Street
bridge. The Yiddish theater
used to be right here
on your block, she says,
when the trees were still
light green. That's where
Gershwin and Berlin
started out. Nature's first
green is gold. That's
Robert Frost. When
we part, she asks if I drink
wine. Not usually, but
occasionally. Then my
love comes by with
a bottle of red wine
and I drink a thimble full.
Tipsy, I touch the edge
of his clavicle, and he says,
Oh, don't do that.
It's much too exciting.

ANIMAL ORCHESTRA

Riding home through the park.
The trees shelter not just me,
but many who have their heads
bowed, drunken and collapsing,
homeless, mentally ill, addicted,
slouching on benches, men
without families, mothers
and fathers long gone or never
there. Home, my love is waiting.
I kiss him spontaneously
and he kisses me back. A toad's
music is a communal shelter
and Bernie Krause's animal
orchestra tonight in this corner
of the globe includes the guys
upstairs talking and giggling
and in the background bird-like
sounds of people passing on the street.

THE WHOLE STORY

Jury duty this morning.
Promptly dismissed,
so I buy an ivy at Saifee's
and mount a big hook
to hang it so the leaves
drift downward. At lunch
Mook asks if I'm seeing
my ex again. Yes, I say
and my grown son
is very quiet. We're
in a zone, I say, where
the players reappear
and score in the blink
of an eye, only to drift
back into the game's
natural flow. Esther laughs
and says, You're in love
with him and you should
write about these diverging
desires. Now I'm drifting
with the long awaited
cleanup of the Gowanus
Canal, and Mr. Mitchell's
solar-powered cell-phone
charger and its eight
charging tentacles
sprouting in the middle,
a kind of holy grail
to help us stay connected.

IN A ROCK SHELTER

In France, researchers
have discovered illustrations
of female anatomy
dating back 37,000 years.
Since then human beings
have used their brains
to figure out how to avoid
this constant scampering
around to find food, obtain
shelter, escape predators.
In the laundromat, a couple
folds a sheet, locking their
eyes and joining the corners
over and over until it's
folded into a small rectangle
and placed into a basket.
It's chilly today, I say
to a homeless man. Can I
pay for a cab to take you
to the shelter. I didn't ask
for your help, he says.
I'm offering anyhow. Lady,
the shelter on 30th Street
doesn't open until midnight.
Just before midnight, while
some of us are asleep,
the president's plane lifts off
toward Afghanistan.

BODIES IN RELATION

With the economic crisis
a Serbian woman says
she'll do anything necessary
to survive, even sell her
kidneys or her liver, whatever.
In a noisy restaurant
on Avenue of Americas,
Martine says, We'll never
know exactly what Gertrude
Stein did with the Vichy
collaborators. And Barbara,
you're losing too much
weight. Everyday eat
a little bit more. Despite
the noisy protests, Bank
of America shareholders
have signed a pay package
for their chief executive
for $7 million. Why should
we not also enjoy an original
relation to the universe, asks
Emerson. In Washington Square,
the baby hawks stretch out
their wings catching a little
wind and flapping vigorously.

RAINING ALL DAY

Coughing on the street
after teaching coughing again.
Lost another four pounds.
Must write a book some day,
called *Cough*. Clear and quiet
on the subway, then the climb up
to the street and two blocks
of coughing. Almost always
coughing in the rain. At St Marks
John Godfrey holds out his hands,
now arthritic. We older poets
hold each other in our words.
When I climb into bed, the guys
above us pull out their bed
and it rolls noisily across the floor.
I want to remember my dreams,
but this anti-coughing drug
makes me sleep so deeply
that when I stand up, I'm sleep
walking. In the morning, like
Mark Teixeira, I must admit
that this noisy cough has not
improved. John Cage says about
noise that it does not have to
disturb. When we really listen,
we will find it fascinating.

TWICE IN ONE LIFETIME

After copulating, the male's
pedipalp breaks off in the female
spider and forms a plug,
preventing other orb spiders
from fertilizing her. Then
she eats her mate. In the 90s,
there was the tech bubble
and after that the housing bubble.
What looks in a still photo
like a very delicate glass
bulb is in fact a bubble.
A big bubble is suspended
above me in the middle
of the room. I watch it drift
over the bed. Then I stand up
and reach out. There's a spider
inside the bubble. When it pops,
I wake up. My love says,
It's Anancy the trickster. Shortly
thereafter, an elderly man drifts
toward Central Park where
a few hours later he's found
sleeping on a bench near the zoo.

SUMMER

FIRST OFF

First the beautician maps
your scalp, then the machine
shoots streams of warm water
and foam shampoo from its
28 nozzles. My head's in suds
when my love texts and asks
if I can sit in his car while
he carries boxes upstairs.
The ginko leaves twinkle back
and forth. His long fingers
hold the steering wheel.
Uptown, a pet raccoon comes
too close to the window's edge
and even his long claws are
unable to save him. Then
it's raining and we're walking
through the park under
an umbrella, our voices muted
by the hypnotic sound of large
drops hitting the pavement.

EVERY TWIRL FORWARD

It's chilly and the homeless
are wearing coats and huddling
in doorways. Bobby is at the
park gate shivering. Do you
need anything? No. Do you want
a shirt? Ok, he says. At home
I find a jacket, but when I return
he's gone. Home builders report
increases in the number of houses
delivered and sales prices are up.
When a child grows up sheltered
to be homeless is a nightmare
to imagine. But the child who's
never been protected, perhaps
he expects to wander alone.
At dusk, I'm watching a boy
play in the park with a girl.
So fluid. Standing shoulder
to shoulder, they climb the bars
and twirl around on the merry
go round. Same size, same shade,
but she has a puffy pony tail.

ON A STICK

At 4th Ave and 14th Street,
the street vendor is cooking
meat on a stick. Black
smoke pours out of his
stove, blowing into the
intersection with hundreds
of people coughing and
moving together across
the street. Smoke into
the branches of my bronchi.
Wildfires in California
and the smoke so bad
the athlete rolls up his window.
Man, he says, I can't breathe.

THE YOUNG BOY

The young boy pedals his bike
to the beach and tosses a bottle
into the waves with a hand-
written note. With my second
load of Bobbie's *Selected Prose*,
twenty-five pounds on the back
of my bike, heavy and wobbly,
I start pedaling to the post office.
Then I realize that I forgot
to stamp *Media Mail.*
Insufficient postage. Pedal
madly. Please, I beg the man,
Can you look in back? This is
New York City, this is an
immense Post Office, but even
with the rampant shut down
of post offices, even with high
unemployment and lack of
wage increases, he says, Yes.
And thousands of poetic messages
spread in the drift. When his
foot hits the low E pedal,
filling the Cathedral with sound,
Houlihan has a heart attack
and dies the way he always
wanted—playing his organ.

ESPECIALLY

A cab driver tells me
that nine out of ten people
behave rudely, especially
in the morning. Think huff,
or evil-eye, or at least
grumble. I practice yoga
beside eighty-two year old
Nancy. Rigorous. Just what
I needed she says. A man's
heart grows a new artery
to feed blood into the other
chambers. At home, my love's
watching a basketball game
and I'm writing in my journal.
When I'm writing, he keeps
talking. When he plays his
guitar, I keep talking. Then
the police swoop in, hornet
like: "Yo! You, come here.
Get against the wall."

AT MARYSIA'S

Kate cuts my hair while
Sylvia gives a manicure
to a beautiful trans-
sexual with a Cher look,
long black hair, black
eye makeup, smooth
skin, hormones working
beautifully. A traditional
Vietnamese living space
is one where you feel
that the sky, earth, animals
and trees exist in perfect
harmony. Really
nice legs and dressed
femme fatale to the nth degree.
The growth spurt will hit
a crest in the next few
decades and it's vitally
important for humanity
to experience a relatively
smooth journey through
this century. Cher's talking
about someone with
traditional ideas about
dating. And all the answers
fall into the right place
at the right time. Her
pencil point never ever
breaks, not even once.

BEHIND THE
ROOM DIVIDER

We're still resting in bed.
Outside the window the men
on the scaffolding are moving
bricks around. Guess what
they're doing now, I hear
someone say. A single rain
drop can weigh 50 times
as much as a mosquito.
The sky's grey and the air thick.
A speedy cable pulls the train
to the top of the roller coaster.
Given the relentless battles
by tech companies to win
new smart phone users,
you'd think that the tiny screen
is the only thing that matters.

WEEDS

A feast of delicious weeds
may be waiting out there
in your backyard. 116 years
ago Friday, Nik Wallenda
became the first man to walk
over the Niagara Gorge.
Someone on the subway says
to another, You've been
Gothamized! Later I go out
walking with my love and then
over to Caravan for a chocolate-
coconut pie. Holding hands,
we stand under the grand old tree
on Seventh Street in front of
the apartment where old
Anthony sits and broadcasts
Frank Sinatra, singing,
It Was a Very Good Year.

A CHUNK OF ICE

about two times the size
of Manhattan breaks free
and sets sail off Greenland.
My shoe falls off while
peddling across Canyon
in Boulder, my hip a little
tight from riding the wrong
size bike with too much
pressure on the quads
and knees. Tight and stable,
the candidates fight over
three percent of the electoral.
The pressure rising with
sweltering temperatures,
lack of rain and the largest
corn crop in generations.
Walking the bike while
my step-mother talks
on the cell about a two-
year-old at the beach tripping
on hot charcoals loosely
covered with sand, the baby
badly burned. My throat's raw
from the smoky afternoon
air, perfect for acoustic
transmission—the particulates
stimulating a sound channel.
While north of Colorado
Springs, some are fleeing
a blizzard of ash and smoke,
I'm coasting downhill
when it starts to rain.

BEHIND THE
POETICS BUILDING

I'm reading *The Times*
on my cell. Big black crows
caw. When I caw back they
get louder. Crows are rarely
found alone and cawing is
a sign of danger. A bush
scrapes my back and then
a mosquito starts buzzing
around my neck. Waves
of migrants leave Siberia
to come to the Americas.
8.5% of Native American
DNA belongs to other races.
In the auditorium, Bobbie
reads from *Back to Texas,*
her mother drawling on
about how to cook liver.
Out too late, I look into
the mirror at my tired face.
All in the same family
even the oil cartel looking
for the mirror image of
rich oil deposits in West
Africa under the oceans
off Latin America where
the land masses first split apart.

WHERE BOULDER LIES

The smoke from the fires blow
into the cavern and then it settles
down and stays here. That's why
I'm coughing. The Buranovskiye
Babushi, the Grandmothers
of Buranovo, sing and dance their
way to worldwide fame, bringing
water lines into their village.
In the Naropa auditorium, we dance
wildly, hundreds dancing, a closing
thing. Ecstatic. In a movie theater
in Aurora, a few weeks later
after midnight, the dark knight
cometh, a masked killer attacking
spectators. In Mushara, with
limited resources, the mostly
gentle sentient elephants begin
fighting with each other. Accidentally,
a broker's software sets off millions
of trades, and an older student
wants to send Bobbie his manuscript.
He sees her fragility and still
he asks. Perhaps he too feels
the pressure of time. She smiles,
I'm sorry, dear, I don't do that.

ANSELM HOLLO

Anselm Hollo is very thin,
frail and barely able to stay
awake. Between his legs
on the blanket a white cat
curls up. Anselm reaches down
and scratches the cat's back
with one long finger. He smiles
and the cat stretches out,
coiling her tail over his leg
and then she falls asleep
and so does Anselm, his mouth
wide open. A wisp of a flower,
speedwell is so frail it's almost
unnoticeable, five tiny striped
purple petals, hiding close
to the ground. Bobbie's on her
knees beside him, stroking
his arm, while Maureen and I
are sitting in half lotus on either
side. Remotely piloted aircraft
operators talk to each other
to stay awake. A subway train
derails after the heat stretches
the track. While Anselm sleeps,
we talk about Laurie Anderson
and the last night at Naropa.
Every so often he opens his eyes
a slit and smiles. Back to sleep,
I ask him if he can hear us
talking while he's asleep
and he nods "Yes" with head
and hand. He doesn't seem
that far from death, I say
at lunch, but Bobbie says
his coloring is better this week
and Maureen agrees.

LIMITATIONS

Thanks to the statute of limitations
Pereny, an art forger, continues
to makes meticulous re-creations
of famous artists for far less.
Meticulous and resourceful,
some Egyptians claim the US
plotted to install the Islamist's
presidential candidate. An NBA
player is caught snoozing
with an airline blanket pulled
snugly around his neck. Eating
lunch at the Hungry Toad,
someone says, Did I ever tell you
the story about blankety-blank?
Most of the conflict was because
he was arrogant and a student-
womanizer. I guess poets can be
as mean-spirited, manipulative
or even as sleepy as anyone else
in academia or in the NBA
for that matter, maybe more so.

WHEN I ARRIVE

Boulder is sizzling, 100 plus
degrees and so dry I can smell
the wildflowers, I mean wildfires,
outside the city. Dry conditions
over much of the nation's bread
basket will lead to higher food
prices. Hot dry weather is making
massive dust storms in Arizona.
Scarcity of water also threatens
power plants and gas and oil
production. Food supplies are
at risk. Bernanke says the economy
is stuck in the mud. Then it starts
raining and the drought is over.
Monsoon and each day there is
more and more water and mud
slides develop in areas where
the fires have burnt out the ground
cover. Biking is a challenge.
When damp, my seat slides down
and when I stop to adjust,
zap down again. When unable
to extend, my long legs can't
engage the necessary muscles.
On Sunday, the rain stops
and the sun is blazing again.
I hang my bedding on a line.
As we drive away, the sheets
are flapping in the breeze.

THE WAY OF QI

Sitting on a bench behind
the Krishna tree, we talk
about how trees know how
to grow in particular directions
so to maintain balance. Three
young men and a woman play
their guitars and a trumpet.
One of them starts singing:
I keep hanging on. We search
on our cells for the songwriter.
Simply Red—once a young man
and ten albums later a middle-
aged guy. Under the Krishna
tree my cell rings. A friend has
cirrhosis and hepatitis and
didn't know it. Follow your
spine with your breath, from
your tailbone to the occipital
ridge of your scull. A spacecraft
is currently speeding toward
a close encounter with Pluto,
and Dr. Stern warns, Get used to
planets unlike Earth ruling.
While writing this poem, I'm
under a cotton sheet with tiny
blue flowers and green polka dots
and the guys upstairs are softly
opening their bed. The cars rev up
mid block and then rush past us.

A BEDOUIN MAN

A Bedouin man isn't certain
whether joining a revolt was
life's proudest moment or its
ruination. The object in your
pocket is a tracking device
that just happens to make calls.
Just perch the clock near the bed
and put your phone on the stand
and it will record your sleep
patterns. Hello. Good night.
The days are going so quickly.
Perhaps we perceive quickness
more in our busy lives than
people did in previous centuries.
Yesterday, Americans used
their sizable advantage to run
others ragged. We lay the child
down into his bed and find
each other under the sheet.
Now with four arms, four legs
and two heads, we circulate qi.
Then the arm starts turning
sideways in a gentle curve, tracing
an S shape, the thumb heading
up as the palm turns parallel,
our bodies and souls parallel.
Oh, the grief of separation.
Don't think, dear, stay here.

THE MOST MUNDANE,
THE MOST

With light there's momentum
and thus a propulsive force
is implicit in the basic equations
of electro-magnetism. Long
exposure from the slow shutter
app creates trails of light
A comet's tale, blown by sunlight.
Little particles that carry energy
and momentum. In the house
there's a painting of Julie
when she was a young child,
with no eyes and light brown
straight hair. Instead of those
beautiful dreds of today. Or
the red African scarf wrapped
around her head. Or the gold
high heels she wore the night
before last. An eye stopper.
When right-handed people
move their eyes up and to the left
in response to a question, they
may be picturing a one hundred
year old Galapagos tortoise
dying. Gentle and trusting—Once
they dominated the land until they
were mercilessly hunted down.
Om nama shivaya Lonesome George.
Om Shantih. I put my suitcase
in the car and drive to Detroit,
the ends of my back bumper
loose and flying out like wings.

NOT ONE ORIOLE

I pour straight cleaning fluid
on the floor and scrub it. A snake
plant topples over—forty-four
years old, Jean says. A snake can
turn the simple act of drinking
into a gymnastic feat. Every cell
is new but with a forty-four year
old memory. De-regulation:
It's a chimera peddled in large part
by snake oil salesmen disguised
as billionaire plutocrats. I'm on
my knees clipping a big patch
of three foot high spearmint.
Smells lovely but into a waste bag
it goes. Up and down the spiders
run this and that way as we pull up
dry stems from last year. A single
slender green leaf spears the air
when a teenage girl in Guwahati,
India steps out of Club Mint
after an evening out with friends.
A group of forty surround her,
beating and stripping her.
Then the police and the TV crew
show up. A colonel in New York
state remotely flies his drone
videoing his intended targets
as they go about their daily lives,
7000 miles away in Afghanistan.
At night, Jean sits in her recliner
clipping text and photos until 3 am.
I'm lying on some cushions on her
back porch, and the air smells
like spearmint as I drift into sleep.

FINE PARTICLES

As a child, our house was full
of soot particles, both parents
active smokers. As a young
girl, after my mother died
I would cry for her at night.
Google is working on fixing
the vulnerability that led to
the disclosure of your data.
Scientists report that an Inca
girl who lived 500 years ago
suffered from a bacterial lung
infection just before she died.
In my twenties I was still
crying. Liver qi stagnation
from your mother's death,
your whole family suffers,
the doctor says. You lose
everyone in your life. The lungs
are your particular weak area.
Finally emotional explosions
are only a provoking cough,
yawn or misfired joke away.

HAND IT OVER

The sole purpose of gazing at tantric
paintings is to achieve a more acute
level of awareness. A color blind
artist sees colors through sound.
In the park a group of Chinese women
practice qi gong. An older Spanish
speaking couple plays paddle ball,
and three African American men
lift up and muscle around and over
the bars. On 92.9 a guy is talking
about how there's not a single mention
of the color blue, but Homer was big
on color. The ancient Greeks didn't
see blue or make that distinction.
My love says there is no word for
blue in Zulu either. Worker termites
in French Guiana carry backpacks
full of blue crystals—when attacked,
they rupture and the secretion is deadly.
The freedom and opportunity promised
in the constitution for working people
has been handed over to corporations,
but the hue of blue may grow deeper
with an increase in democratic voters.

THE SPEED OF LIGHT

A magnificent frigate sea bird
lives in the Galapagos,
the blue-footed booby.
In Untemyer Gardens a lion's
magnificent calm stone face
is smeared with graffiti.
In Mountain Lion OS you can
now zoom in or out of your
document just by pinching
or spreading two fingers.
An invisible energy field slows
the particles down. Without it
all elementary forms of matter
would zoom around at the speed
of light. Quick zooms, abrupt
edits and a restless camera
accelerate the momentum.
We're sauntering along Avenue A
while our boy zooms ahead
on his scooter, so fast and
graceful, slipping his right
foot behind his left and then
leaning toward the left to go
around the corner. Pennsylvania
is now leaning democratic,
and with the recession, more
than a few young adults are
leaning on their elderly parents.

I MEET LEWIS
FOR LUNCH

I meet Lewis for lunch
at Angelica's. We eat wee
dragon bowls with mu tea.
Then I bike over to Santo's
in the rain to make copies
of my poetic prose book.
A narrow shop on Ninth
Street with room for three
at a time, a narrow margin,
that's all that's needed.
We wait in line while 150
tons of glittering plastic
beads spill overboard
in a typhoon, fish and
albatross passing them
down the throats of their
babes. Buttons for sale
at Santo's, made by my
friend Sally. *Welcome
to McHattan*. I buy one.

UNNAMEABLE

In the graveled garden
behind Unnameable Books
Patricia Spears Jones
is reading her poems.
A large fish fly (or
something like that)
is perched on the wire
overhead. Glass-shattering,
flip-flopping, like
the mayor of London
sliding down a zip wire.
In the middle of the crowd,
a poet lights up, nervously
flicking his cigarette.
I read my poems, stumble
and drop my cell phone,
the glass shattering.
Something clearly is
going awry. Underground
subway construction
makes windows up above
break. I cough. Patricia
coughs. It'll all go back
to normal, I think, without
going into a conflict zone.
Then another lights up,
then another and another.
Finally David K asks
the smokers just for now
kindly please go to the rear.

ACROSS THE TABLE

Luke reaches across the table
and knocks his beautiful lego
ship onto the floor. It breaks
into tiny pieces and he starts
crying. The captain of the *Titanic*
went down with the ship. Usually
women and children die first.
The Lion King is on TV.
When the father lion is dying,
Lolo's cries, I don't wanna watch this.
A whale circles below his prey
and a spectacular hacking takes
place on icloud. Sitting on the
side of the tub, I tell the boys
about a horse that escaped
from his carriage this morning
and galloped right through
Columbus Circle. Four blocks
of freedom. Then I put my feet
into the tub and they joyfully
scrub them. Love them, feet, boys
and low scrub as far as far can be.

DIPPING AND SWAYING

As he buttons his pocket, he says,
I'm black so I need to carry my ID.
Young men dribble and shoot,
block and run. A young Chinese
girl swings around the bars,
trying some gymnastic moves
she saw on TV. The monkey
grasshopper moves side to side
to judge distance before a jump.
I think twice sometimes about
driving together on Long Island,
he says—Crazy right wingers
there, too. Some dude is playing
Spanish guitar in the park.
Skinny monkeys don't live
any longer than bigger ones.
More ultra right wing militias
since the election of Obama,
but on the wing, Graham Zusi
flicks the ball ahead to Teal Bunbury.
So why not? the man says
while I stand still and watch him
tango with an invisible partner
in the middle of the park, a big smile
and his body dipping and swaying.

ALL THAT
DISCARDED STUFF

We go to Brooklyn
and buy some expensive
live mouse traps. Put
cheese and peanut butter
inside. And wait. No
mice visiting in this box,
but all over the kitchen
little trails. Have you
ever thought about
the data trail you leave
behind as you go about
your ordinary daily life?
All that discarded stuff
is certainly there, but
it's submerged, hidden
up and down the water
column, sometimes
thousands of feet deep.

ACROSS MY EYES

Strip mined or boiled loose
underground. Pipe it. Burst it.
One million gallons of crude
bitumen into the Kalamazoo
River. In the house with my
muscles pumped up, I turn off
the news and then my love's
guitar sends a chord across
my eyes and I drift into—
let's go to bed. I hear him
showering. Then he's doing
qi gong by candlelight.
He climbs into our bed,
saying he's sending me qi.
His hands are burning hot.
Overhead, smog-forming
nitrogen oxide and sulfur
dioxide drifting eastward from
mid-western power plants.

SUPERIOR MUSCLES

I'm following Kayin
as he scoots around
the basketball courts.
I can feel the plastic
of the back panel flex
against the circuit board
inside my back pocket.
Mexico may very well
flex its superior muscles,
but flex-fuel vehicles
can run on any blend.
A young Russian girl,
very agile, whip whap
and she's back and forth
across the bars while
her sister is chubby
and insecure and quickly
falls to the ground.
I pull-up a quarter inch
with a little flex of some
muscle in my shoulder.
Hopeless. While men
have a bit more muscle
mass than women,
usually the one with
firepower triumphs.

DESPITE

Despite the steady
discharge of treated
sewage water into
the Hudson, currently
it's considered safe
for human contact.
Smoking is something
else one does now,
in some places
on the sly, the butt
cupped inside one's hand,
but not in the East Village.
Here smokers
clutter the edges
of the sidewalks.
Through a tunnel of
smoke, I hold my breath
while thousands
line up elsewhere,
waiting for bread or
deportation deferrals.

SURVIVAL SKILLS

While tropical storm Isaac
gains strength, churning
toward the Gulf Coast,
today in Tompkins Square,
a group of African-American
teens are slugging each
other in the belly. Young
testosterone, my friend says,
they must stay strong
to survive on the street.
To improve the strength
of my upper arms, I follow
my coach's instructions.
For doing the chataranga
pushup, he says, you need
to strengthen tricep
and seratus anterior.
Those from the Shang
dynasty say that bear paw
should not be eaten in such
a rush. So slow it down.

FAMILY ECONOMICS

In *Because I was Flesh,*
Edward Dahlberg narrates
his philo-mythic-analytic
mind easily segueing into
the mind of his mother,
Lizzy, a lady barber
in Kansas City. Like a
jazz jam session, whatever
here and there, wherever
the mind goes the mind
goes, a lettuce factory
in California where robots
pack boxes beside human
workers. Why did I let her
die alone, he wonders.
Self critical, he never says
what I want to say—She
put you in an orphanage,
Ed, at eleven years old
and left you for seven years.
Say it louder. Maybe in the
1980s, the suitcase-size
boom box was a necessity.
Bigger was better. Dahlberg's
box was ecstasy, metaphor
and philosophy. After
reading, I clean the closet
and toss out three years'
worth of empty boxes,
making space for someone
else to hang his clothes.

I CLOSE MY BOOK

Stand up and drop my
new replacement phone
into the toilet. There are
apps to help you find
your phone. Despite
advances in technology,
many fall unrecorded.
In Queens, a policeman
trips over a scooter
while chasing a peacock.
The inmates from six
halfway houses escape
NYC, and in Russia,
the police corner
a woman protesting
at the Turkish embassy.
In a yoga class, we
listen to a recording
of Spitsbergen bowhead
whales singing, screeching
and whistling. A system
of brackets and gears
adjusts the height
and angle of our elbows.
A tourist films the NYC
police shooting a man
with a knife. No more
shooting to wound.
There's a lot more to say
but after some profound
conclusions, a deep back
bend and after Angie's
dog curls up beside me,
I promptly fall asleep.

SO MUCH
HAS HAPPENED

Tonight we go to a film
by D'Suisa on Obama.
Passengers on buses
rumbling down Fifth
Avenue were yelling,
What an asshole!
I couldn't sit through it.
Shut up! I muttered.
We no longer expect
to hear the truth
so blatant falsehoods
are possible. Later
my love is lying
beside me. It's after
midnight when he says,
Liver stagnation
that's your problem
but sometimes you're
    really funny.

THE A TRAIN
TO BROOKLYN

A young woman carrying
a skate board asks if I know
where Pratt is. Well
I do if I'm walking,
but not from here. A man
in a business suit says
to another, "I am deeply
concerned about the direction
of the company." A tall
young man in a baseball
cap has a red cord running
into his pocket. Another
woman is reading Sister
Souljah's *The Coldest Winter*
Ever and it's blistering hot
today. The woman beside me
says to her friend, "He
broke her fire-escape window
and took a big ole African
violet she was growing for
twelve years." In the neon
underground buzz I miss
my stop, backwards eleven
to Clinton-Washington.

WHEN I AM

When I am
spraying Kayin
down, he says,
"You're my special
friend, Barbara.
You're like a
mom." I say,
"And you
are so lucky
to have so many
people spraying
your body
before you
go to bed, dude."
We laugh.
We laugh a lot.

IN A CITY LIKE THIS

Everyone's on the go,
everyone but the man
sleeping beside the garbage,
his cheek on the cement,
a baseball hat over his face,
people stepping over him.
His sign: I'm a veteran.
Forty years after the US
stopped spraying agent
orange in Vietnam jungles,
we're starting to clean up.
A full moon partly visible
through the trees. When
I climb into bed, my veteran
lover is sleeping in the chair.
I ask him if he's coming
to bed and he squints and
says, I know what I want.
When another person is stern
with me, my heart gets heavy.
Genny says, Yoga is a healing
art. Just by doing it, you
open blockages in the body.
There's always the possibility
of taking a seven and a half
mile walk, lying flat with
pressurized inflatable cuffs,
hooked up to a heart monitor.
Inflate, deflate. Someday
we'll spray saltwater into the air
and make big soft salt clouds
to reflect dangerous sunlight
and reverse global warming.
I close my eyes and imagine
deep salutations to the sun.

FALL

PUSH ME. I PUSH YOU

As the yawning gap narrows,
one candidate still has
a double digit lead.
And Post-it notes flutter
in the Brooklyn breeze.
Today we turn methane
into plastic, into methane,
then plastic again.
A good practice to stay
balanced and even-keeled
while dusk comes and
comes. Even electric blue
pants won't stay in the
fast lane. We ride without
a helmet, dangerous,
nonetheless, just to feel
the breeze in our hair.
I'm safe in bed writing
with a nightlight, the over-
head fan on low and a group
of men laughing loudly
as they pass from one bar
to another, our boy fast
asleep while my love is
reading on his tablet with
the windows open wide
and a cool breeze occasionally
wafting through the room.

NOT THAT ONE

A guy with a block of ice,
shaves it and pours lemon-
basil-sugar syrup into our cups.
On a bench near the 7th Street
park entrance, Kayin and I
sit beside three German tourists.
We are slurping away when
they light up. Keep your
eyes on that one. Influenzas
are explosive. I warn them
they'll get a ticket for smoking
in a public park. If I breathe
smoke, I start to cough.
For centuries in Cuba they
rolled cigarettes from raw
twisted tobacco leaves.
So one twin gets a disease,
the other doesn't necessarily.
In this park, homeless, addicts,
the mentally disturbed and
the punks are ticketed for
smoking. Some punks band
together and sleep in groups.
Today a young woman is
standing between two cars.
She shimmies down her pants
and poops in broad daylight.
Behind her, the leaves on
the scholar trees are flickering.

LOOK AT HIS CALVES

Tired without his nap,
little Logan is running
with his feet almost entirely
off the ground. On scooters
the boys zoom around
the edge of a parking lot,
Logan races behind them.
It's in his DNA—a horse
has four feet off the ground
at a trot. Today an exuberant
pizza maker lifted Obama
two feet off the ground.
I sit behind Logan on
the floor and we watch
Harry Potter. Tell me
Gramma, he whispers,
what's happening now?
His brother is at attention,
intently watching Hagrid
and his dog, Fluffy, his eyes
sparkling blue with
a quirky sideways smile.
Someday they'll both
be six and a half feet tall.

FOR THE FIRST TIME

For the first time in many
years or maybe the first time
ever, I make several baskets.
Then a bike cuts through
the courts with a little white
dog propped up in the basket,
dressed like ET. Behind
him a group of adolescent
boys and one slightly older
teenage girl run into the court,
swearing and edging toward
a little boy. His father moves
closer and they back away.
In the everglades, foxes,
rabbits and other mammals
are vanishing, while baby
pythons proliferate. We follow
the boy as he scoots around
the big elms heading south
toward Avenue A and 7th Street.

ACCIDENTAL INTENTIONS

Was it an accident that
the police shot a rubber bullet,
a taser and ten real bullets
into an emotionally disturbed
young man's body? To wound
rather than kill, an idea from
the past. Depends on whose
past you're talking about,
my love says as we ride
our bikes along the East River
to Battery Park. Twice right
in front of me, Kayin falls off
his bike, but he's quickly up
and riding with his helmet
bobbing, straight to Riverside
Terrace and across the highway
to a steel tube as high as
a five-story building. Rocks
are the wobbly steps to the top.
Whoosh down they go into
a bed of sand. I watch them
both from the top. If you can't
breathe or finish what you start,
no one's going in there for you.
     So take care.

ON ANY GIVEN DAY

There are 650,000 people
in the US without a place
to sleep. When we wake up
sparrows are busy pecking
around the base of the locust
tree. Kayin comes to yoga
with me and draws pictures
of hummingbirds. When
hummingbirds fly backwards,
they still have a very upright
body posture. Animals frequently
tangle horns with each other.
The boy is wearing a hat
with big horns and rattling eyes.
Everybody knows the animal
is telling outright lies, still
he gets 51% of the poll. Why
don't their brains turn to pudding?
At night, Kayin asks,
Does your body keep working,
Barbara, when you go to sleep?

VERY WINDY AND CLEAR

I'm coasting downhill around
the corner on my bike.
Well, it's more like swaying
with the back tire almost flat.
Last night everyone on TV,
even the President was
swaying to Stevie Wonder
under a portrait of Washington.
Even though the candidate
loves big bird, he's not going
to support public television
and he's not going to tax
the rich either. They're
doing just great, he says.
At Union Square pick up
a paper and read that
Barbara Blum died this week.
In the 80s she fought
and rescued mentally disabled
and neglected children
from Willowbrook State
School in Staten Island.
The neighbors near the group
homes, pelted her with eggs
and one person even broke
her nose. Some children were
saved, but now not enough
beds for the mentally ill.
They fill the prisons and
wander the streets, sleeping
on benches in Tompkins
Square and after midnight,
on the sidewalks, along
fences and in the nooks and
crannies outside the cathedrals.

LED ZEPPELIN TOUCHES

down in NYC for a quick reunion
and on the bus a middle-aged woman
loudly scolds an adolescent for combing
her hair and letting it touch her jacket.
The republican doesn't want to come off
as a scold, and the ecologist refuses
to scold the bug-fearing masses. Instead
he sits quietly inside a forest circle,
listening and breathing. An old woman
is unsteady in the bus but no one offers
her a seat. Some kind of planetary thing—
At the bottom and in the middle, they say
American society is fraying just as a small
earth-like planet is found in the Alpha
Centauri, a triple star system, our closest
neighbor, 4.4 light-years away. When
the melatonin hour arrives and the moon turns,
like dancers rotating around a yogi split,
a leg as a geometric compass, we go deeply
into our shared intimate circle of sleep.

ALL ABOUT STYLE

We're in a traffic jam on the LIE
when my lover says, You don't
have any style. You don't even
know what style is. I blink.
If you don't like me Lord Dude,
why are you here? And he laughs
real loud. When I was little
I used to run around outside
with no shirt on. On Sundays,
I wore patent leather shoes.
Got my first garter belt at ten.
After my mother died I used to
wear her old nylon stockings
and her fringe leather jacket.
Used to wear panty hose and
high heels. Used to rat my hair
and bleach it blonde like Twiggy.
Allen and I wore the same clothes
and size, our torn levis, tee shirts,
construction boots. Once he bought
a dress for me made from men's ties.
I used to twirl my vintage skirts
at Alvin's Finer. The wines of
Fleurie are light, pretty, feminine
and flowery, but sometimes
I just want to slip into a slip
or a pair of yoga pants. While
I'm stewing inside my body
and my sometimes lover is inside
his headset, the radio man talks

about Miles and why he didn't
want to do the same old kind
of blue anymore, stylistically
static, he said, second hand.
And the funny thing is, we
both kind of love *Kind of Blue*.

HURRICANE SANDY

When floodwaters rise,
websites and trees fall
and hospitals flood. A man
in Brooklyn was in his bed
when a tree fell on him.
Outside the window, the trees
bend over and bang into each other.
In the dark, in our small
studio, I wish for a little closet
with a candle. So I brave
the wind, stepping over piles
of branches blowing from the park.
Cafe Yaffa's the same as ever,
funky and warm, with a noisy
blender, a radio, and a few
other customers. When the wind's
a little calmer, I hug in close
to the buildings on Avenue A
until I'm home in our three hundred
and fifty square feet, with candles
and flashlights, my love playing
his guitar and Kayin building
lego space ships, while I'm
propped up in bed, reading
essays on greed and captivity
in Melville's *Benito Cereno.*

BIRDS DODGE

Birds dodge hurricane winds,
adjust their courses, or use
the wind to propel themselves
forward. Without power,
old folks suffer the most.
Under a coat and two blankets
101 year old Pao Chu Hsieh
lost her breath and her life.
Law-makers are unsettled by
Democratic victories and folks
at Bellevue are unsettled
as they try to relocate their
dislocated patients. When
we go out walking, the wind
unsettles my hair, the top
of my head cold. It's as if
the hurricane thundered
through the city, started a
devastating fire and then
shifted the season from fall
to winter. In Kenya, Qumquat,
a forty-four year old matriarch
elephant heard gunshots,
then she thundered over,
falling to the ground, her face
cut off and her ivory stolen.

IN THE BASEMENT

Petro's mopping floors.
Friday more work, he says,
flood water still everywhere.
In Bellevue Hospital water
could be heard pouring
through the elevators.
In Arizona, facing her shooter,
Ms. Giffords has a sling on
her arm. The judge wonders
about the social utility
of allowing citizens to have
magazines with thirty bullets.
I sling my yoga mat over my
shoulder, throw dvds
and books in my bag and walk
past the now leafless mother
gingko, storm battered papers
and leaves scattered over
the basketball courts.
Two guys are working out
on the bars even though
it's frigid cold. Across the street
to the library, a week late
but because of the hurricane
no charge, the clerk says.
Are these for your grandchildren?
No, my boyfriend's son is
here on the weekends, same
age as my grand children.
Lucky me, I get to do it again.

PHYSICAL THERAPY

After the storm, biking uptown
on First Avenue. Let your shoulders
fall down, hug them into your ribs.
The FTC shuts down robo-calling
Rachel. My cell rings, This is
Bridget from cardholder services.
Stop at NYU hospital, the lobby
crowded with police and con ed
workers, five feet of water
in the basement. Up river,
raw sewage in the waterways.
Patients relocated and my doctor
now operating at Lenox Hill.
Someone will call to re-schedule.
No refunds for metro-cards even
though the subway was shut down.
Light traffic. Not enough gas
to go around. Betting on natural gas
Shell is building a giant vessel
that'll float over a gas field
off the coast of Australia. A sagging
job market and mounting student
debt, young people squeezed out
of college. I squeeze between a bus
and a truck, and then I'm coasting
downhill downtown on Second Avenue.

WHEN I OPEN MY EYES

A knuckleboom loader plucks up
the mighty oak as if it were a twig.
Dust in my sinuses, throat, lungs.
I lie on the floor, propped up
on pillows covered with a quilt.
At a lookout where Kerouac
once sat, a small seated silhouette
watches for a spark. My acupuncturist
takes burning moxa-mugwart,
lifts up the blanket and holds it
over particular points on my legs,
arms and stomach. Over 100
burned bodies are lined up
on the floor of Tazreen Fashions
in Bangladesh. Bus-size boilers
from Texas prop up our steam
systems and bring heat into cold
dark public housing. I bike home
from Union Square in the icy rain—
covered in plastic, my glasses steaming,
rain rolling down my cheeks, cars
and pedestrians cutting here and there.
In the long run, so they say, the ice
and the middle class will slowly disappear.

ON THE TOPSIDE

There's a layer of snow
and the wind is whistling,
a layer of uncertainty
for millions without lights.
The guy with the gold paper
crown in Union Square station
is singing, well it's more like
moaning, and we are transfixed.
Grasshoppers produce their
mating song by rubbing a file
on their hind legs against
a protruding vein on their front
wings. A woman is shattered
by my comments on her
manuscript. I could have lied.
The rate at which the universe
is birthing stars has fallen sharply
and continuously in the last
eleven billion years. Marie
Antoinette moaned her way
to the guillotine and the critic
reports minimal amusement.
Political die-hards in ballrooms
and bars watch election returns,
whooping and moaning. Now
my body is nervous as I measure
the total price tag for all
the damage and then there are
the trees to consider. Sometimes
revision isn't a viable option.

TRY OPENING
THE ZOOM

At Ne's house, Luke and
Kayin are zooming around
on the driveway on scooters,
like jets on the fringes of a
wild-card chase. Collapsing
ground can cause trees
to lean at crazy beautiful
angles. Logan is carrying
around a birthday card that
someone gave him last year.
He's looking into it, smiling
and saying out loud to himself,
This is *my* birthday card.

TODAY IT'S DAMP
AND COLD

But it's supposed to be sixty
on the weekend says the doorman
at 841 Broadway as he leans
over the counter, wearing
a stuffed turkey on his head,
a toy turkey imitating a dead
turkey. At Angelica *Anna Karenina*
is on film and it's as if the actors
are walking from one room
to another and then over the edge
into winter and a new chapter
where our demographic edge
is steadily falling. The council
member says she sent sheaves
of petitions to public officials
warning of storm damage,
possible catastrophe. The film
is more erotic, I think, than Tolstoy
with men carrying their sheaves
in fields of yellow grain, gazing
grain, askance of the panoptic gaze,
like a Van Gogh painting or
Emily passing children for
eternity at recess in the ring.

WINTER

THIS MORNING IN
TOMPKINS SQUARE

More than forty people
in the food line. Not only
are the rents too high but
food prices are escalating, too.
A perverse stroke of urban
planning. Four hulking high
towers in Far Rockaway
with elderly men and women
swaddled in coats and blankets.
After the hurricane,
the pan rack comes loose
from the ceiling, forty
pounds crashing onto the floor.
After the hurricane,
the humidifier flies off
a shelf breaking into pieces.
Cumin seeds everywhere.
As if every loose ball is
a stray animal to be corralled.
A sink full of broken dishes.
Puritans once outlawed
Christmas merriment. Two
space probes crash intentionally
on the dark side of the moon.

UNDER THE SCAFFOLDING

In the afternoon, the markets
are quiet as traders await
a budget deal. In the evening,
on the street a man is yelling.
The sounds of people we are
close to can bring back
an extraordinary intimacy.
A drunken and rowdy group.
I keep falling into a deep sleep.
Trees felled by a storm usually
do not have deep roots, expanding
horizontally instead into a flat
plate like mass. At 1:30 am,
there are still people on the street.
Then it's quiet, the snow thick
against the sidewalk. I hear
a high-pitched hum in my left ear
and the same voices return
louder than before. A police car
and an ambulance. Flashing lights.
I can't see the man but he's
saying again that he didn't do it.
A stomping hollering bluesman.
He was my friend, he yells,
and I wouldn't do that to a friend.

COMING TO YOUR CITY

In Park Slope, a red-tailed hawk
sits on a window ledge, devouring
a freshly killed squirrel. Dogs
can't distinguish between reds
and greens. I am running a fever,
have a head ache, need to sleep,
but can't lie down and breathe
at the same time. Feel like drinking
a quart of dark red cough syrup.
A character in a virus coming
to your city or town soon.
The economics of austerity
play out exactly according to script.
Ok Einstein so you miss spending
Christmas Eve with the boys.
You are not sleeping in an iron
lung tonight. Little Logan is pacing
around, Linnee says, holding
his guitar tightly to his heart.
On the phone, he says, This is
just what I wanted. Red. How did
you know, Gramma, I wanted red?

NEW YEAR'S EVE

Mr. Zlobin writes a book
about Americans and how we
interrogate complete strangers.
Two men interrogate a woman,
one in gentle, soothing tones,
while the other fires staccato
bursts of accusatory questions.
Her husband is reading a magazine
called *Wired* when she repeats
her question. He snarls and
commands that she be still.
To issue spoken commands
on most Androids, you must
tap the microphone gently.
In Russia, children are raised
by their grandmothers.
An average mother would never
dream of leaving her child
with a teenager. She says
it seems as if he doesn't care
about her. He stands up
in a wild sea storm in the Gulf
of Alaska, where a Shell Oil
drilling rig runs aground
with 139,000 gallons
of diesel fuel. The unified
command will be monitoring
the situation. It's midnight
with fireworks when he walks
out while his wife is pleading
with him to stay. Frankenstein's
monster on occasion turns
out to be rather sweet.

GRAND BOYS

Two little boys stand at my bedside,
while I'm recovering from surgery
and unable to speak. Lung health
and low hip bone density correlate
with light smoking by age 19.
Logan looks at me and then slowly
walks into the kitchen. A day later,
he comes again with one hand
on his hip, the other pointing toward
the living room, Do you mean
to tell me that *Mookie* is sleeping
in there? Some teenagers are
terminally hip, but Logan is only
three years old. Luke comes
to the side of my bed and asks me
to play legos with him. A tennis
player digs his heel deep into the court,
and play is suspended as a group
of officials stare at the hole. When
his father was murdered for ideas
about math and the Koran, the only
Arab American to play in the MLB
started driving a cab in Tucson.
What if we all take an oath to heal
and protect each other? Luke stands
beside me. If I rub my hands
together like this and hold them
over your tummy to heal you,
then will you come and play legos?

AIRBORNE

In a birdman suit a woman can stay
airborne for more than three minutes,
the closest thing to engineless flight
we've ever experienced. Shot by
a boy, another boy is slick
with sweat and barely conscious.
He groans and looks into the eyes
of a passerby before he dies.
Walking very slowly along First
Avenue with my body tilted forward.
European nations are tilting toward
offering at least diplomatic support.
Before the judge, the man keeps
his hands in his jean pockets
and his head tilted down. Behind
me the green slick bike path is still
wet from morning rain. Feeling weak
and vulnerable, I put my bag strap
across my chest so no one can grab it.
A friend once complained about
a woman who was holding her purse
tightly when he passed by. Perhaps
attacked before and so a little hyper
aware, I say. Laughing he pretended
to be sinister. Sometimes we humans
really don't understand each other.

.

TEXT ME PLEASE

The psyche is often well
hidden with social media
building layers of distraction.
*I found your slip hanging
in the bathroom.* Ravi
will never forget the reading
he gave when an elderly
gent shouted, That's not
Ravi Shankar! When
a person feels lonely or
excluded his or her skin
literally becomes colder.
I will sleep with it. Chronic
sleep loss lowers tolerance
for pain. As the lust for
gold skyrockets, the demand
for imitation jewelry
grows by leaps and bounds.
*With us sex is a way
to channel emotions. I could
get lost in you.* Roaming
New York City with his camera,
Leon Levinstein once said,
It's a very lonely occupation
if you want to call it that.

BUNDLING

American is bundling
extra fees while Southwest
is unbundling. I'm
bundled up in a fat coat
while the cold wind
blows in my face.
Chugging along
toward the bus shelter
on Avenue A, I'm
planning to hide from
the wind in the corner,
but when I get there,
a young woman in
a red leather jacket
has already staked it out.
On their wedding day,
many brides choose
to hide their tattoos.
This woman's tattoo
is a vine climbing around
her neck and over her cheek.
I say, We just missed
the bus and she says,
If you miss one, another
will surely come along.

IN A SMALL CLOUD

A poet tells me that he has been ill.
His breath stinks. Unconsciously,
I move backwards. Maybe
I'm repelling, too. When Allen
was dying we were in a restaurant
and people stared at him. His teeth
were falling out. It's hard to be
presentable when you're ill.
Backward doesn't necessarily
mean we are going backwards.
Walking home from the Poetry
Project, I tap my leg and count
while holding my breath. Toe-
tapping rhythms. Today it's
possible to book a round-the-world
air ticket simply by tapping
a smartphone. So cold. Fierce.
Mouth breathing can frost your
lens. I refuse to cough. When
I'm on a mobile device I'm more
likely to be presentable. After
passing through the gate, I start
coughing. Why, the father asks
his son, do you always cry when
you have to do your homework?
I don't know, the boy says.
We're not really going backwards.
We're standing side by side
in a small cloud of our own breath.

OUT OF THE ELEVATOR

I stand on the curb in a gust
of wind. Soon the familiar
rumble will arrive, the light
will change and I'll catch
the Q to Union Square,
carrying fifty pounds of
student folders, moving
with a mass of other bodies,
each going exactly where
she intends. Biking home
on 14th Street, it starts to rain
with gusts as high as 60 miles
per hour. A report on nearly
three million people finds
that those whose body mass
index ranks them as overweight
have less risk of dying
than people with normal
weight. Exhausted, I peel off
my pants and my wet knee-socks
and then fall deeply asleep,
inner walls bristling with
impossible-to-follow strings
of *this* unfathomable reason
and *that* memory connecting
one image with another.

Photo by Cliff Fyman

ABOUT THE AUTHOR

Born in Detroit in 1948, Barbara Henning has lived in New York City since 1983. She is the author of ten books of poetry, *A Swift Passage, Cities and Memory; My Autobiography, A Slow Curve, Detective Sentences, In Between, Me & My Dog, Love Makes Thinking Dark, The Passion of Signs* and *Smoking in the Twilight Bar;* three novels, *Thirty Miles to Rosebud, You, Me and the Insects* and *Black Lace;* and numerous limited edition artist pamphlets, combining photography and writing. She is also the author of a book of interviews, *Looking Up Harryette Mullen* and the editor of *The Selected Prose of Bobbie Louise Hawkins.* She teaches at Long Island University in Brooklyn, where she is Professor Emerita. Her website is www.barbarahenning.com

28443709R00088

Made in the USA
Lexington, KY
15 January 2019